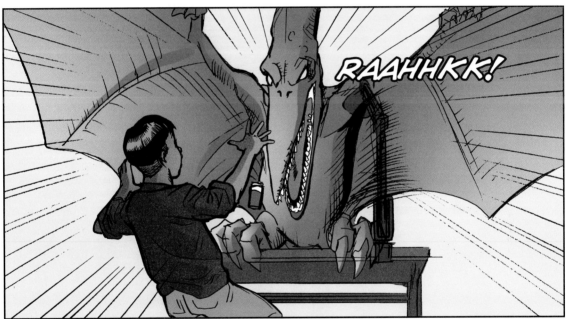

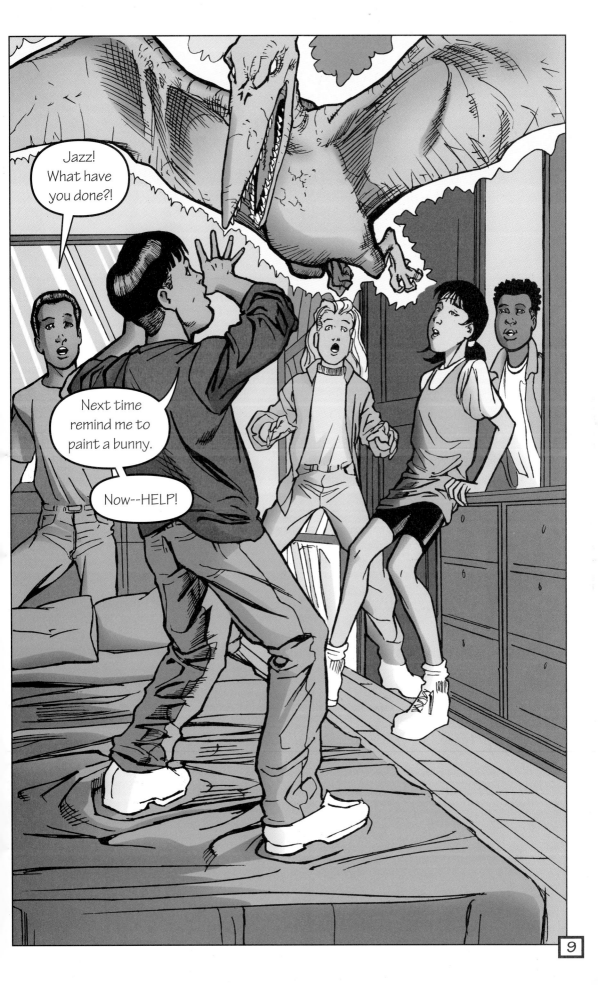

I thought I heard footsteps!

What are you kids doing here? The museum is closing early today.

We came to tell you about Jazz.

Our young **genius** who decided to change the mural without permission?

But he's going to fix it.

Then . . . he'll be back to work on it soon?

Yeah, and he wanted us to tell you that.

He said he really wants to fix the mural. He seems . . . very **determined**.

To Be Continued.